Spring Up Everlasting

WINNER OF THE ADRIENNE BOND POETRY AWARD

Previous Winners

Seaborn Jones, *Going Farther into the Woods than the Woods Go*
(published 2012)

Kelly Whiddon, *The House Began to Pitch*
(published 2013)

Megan Sexton, *Swift Hour*
(published 2014)

Philip Lee Williams, *The Color of All Things: 99 Love Poems*
(published 2015)

Lesley Dauer, *Carnival Life*
(published 2016)

Katy Giebenhain, *Sharps Cabaret*
(published 2017)

Sara Pirkle Hughes, *The Disappearing Act*
(published 2018)

R. T. Smith, *Summoning Shades*
(published 2019)

MERCER UNIVERSITY PRESS

Endowed by

TOM WATSON BROWN
and
THE WATSON-BROWN FOUNDATION, INC.

Spring Up Everlasting

POEMS

WILLIAM WOOLFITT

MERCER UNIVERSITY PRESS
Macon, Georgia
2020

MUP/ P601

© 2020 by Mercer University Press
Published by Mercer University Press
1501 Mercer University Drive
Macon, Georgia 31207
All rights reserved

9 8 7 6 5 4 3 2 1

Books published by Mercer University Press are printed on acid-free paper that
meets the requirements of the American National Standard for Information
Sciences—Permanence of Paper for Printed Library Materials.

Printed and bound in the United States.

This book is set in Garamond.

Cover/jacket design by Burt&Burt

ISBN   978-0-88146-735-2
Cataloging-in-Publication Data is available from the Library of Congress

for Sara

This old land pit, green hole, is filled up
with the bones of all I loved.

~ Irene McKinney

CONTENTS

Spring Up Everlasting

Slurry Spill

near Inez, Kentucky

It could seem like mercy, like good fortune,
a passing over: that when the slurry
breaks the waste pond's bottom, it oozes down
two creeks, not one, divides itself between
Coldwater Fork and Wolf Creek, doesn't rise
very high. *Dead fish, but no people died.*
Like good luck, that the slurry—three hundred
million gallons, thick as pitch, a dark
dirty slop of mud, mercury, arsenic,
debris that's left after the prep plant scrubs
its surfeit of coal—that the slurry comes
into town not as flash flood, grinding surge,
but as low ripples, a foul gummy soup.
The thickest chocolate shake, people say.
*Smells like hydraulic. A slow-moving black
smothering.* Children throw rocks at the creek,
busted cement bricks, old tires, just to find
what else will float. *Around here, you don't
have to be Jesus to walk on water.*

The Sea Turtles of Barra de Parismina

Costa Rica

Volunteers for the community patrol,
two brothers carry shopping bags, grease pens,
and flashlights, walk the moonless beach, seeking
sand that's darker, tilled up, signs of a mother

leatherback dragging herself past the surf-mark,
where the ocean nudges, tongues the shore—
sea-murmur so constant they might not hear panting,
her scooping out the pit-nest where she lays

her clutch of eggs. The older brother repeats
the novena of Our Lord, makes prayers
to Virgen del Carmen, asks for eyes to find
and ears to catch. The younger scans the tall grass

where poachers crouch, inspects the dark sand,
the dark water and sky. And then both spy
a pale-spotted carapace, drop to their knees,
and while she flippers the sand back in, they remove

what feels like fifty jellied ping-pong balls,
take this bounty of eggs to the town criadera,
bury it in the artificial nests they guard at night.
The older brother lights cigarillos, watches

for the hueveros who will come with wire-cutters
and spades unless he pinches himself awake.
The younger eats Pringles, flattens the cans.
They brood in shifts. When the hatchlings pierce

their shells with caruncle-teeth and tunnel up
through sand, the brothers deliver them to the tide,
and set down the generation they carry, drive away
the ghost crabs. Craning their necks, the tortugitos

search for bright pieces of sky, then clamber toward
the low waves that ease them from the sand.

Self Portrait Near the Abandoned
Homeplace on Spruce Run

The creek rain-churned, spring peepers
burrowed in the ooze. My old ones who
planted and worshipped here years back
are lost to me, their names as walnut hulls
stamped into sodden earth, blood-ties
too fine to see, chain ferns, spider webs
on the tenth day of rain. Reach for them,
I find wet sticks, damp cinders that yield
no fire, no curl of smoke. On my hands,
ash smears, stains of wet bark, grooves,
map of a country drifting from memory.
In the water, glimpses of frog, a minnow
of sun, ghosting down, sliver-shaped.

The Wish to Take Sacrament with the
Red Knob Holiness Church

near Gate City, Virginia

Sometimes I want to be joined, folded in,
taken into a body not my own,
changed the way grape juice
from a blue Mason jar and the chewed
saltine cracker dissolve on the tongue,
are transformed in the throat,
in the guts. Sometimes I want to kneel
at the plank bench inside the one-room
church with insurance calendars,
the nativity on velvet, and fly swatters
hanging on the walls, I want
the enjoyment Brother Roy describes,
want to untie my shoe, slip off my sock
while he sets out the dishpans,
while Sister Gladys plugs in
the coffee pot, heats water to mix
with the chilly well-water
pumped outside, water like I imagine
God's spirit to be—clear, moving, free,
silver-bright in the deeps—
while Sister Myrtle arranges towels washed
a hundred times, wrung out, dried
on clotheslines, sun-faded
and raveling, coming undone.

The Extraordinary Rendition of Mohamed Farag Bashmilah

Bagram, Afghanistan

TWO DIGITAL WATCHES

He marks the hours with a prayer chart, a watch with a map of the world. Guards take the watch, tape outside the plexiglass another watch, its straps cut away. Time drags, he doesn't look at the face.

WATER

When given plastic bottles with the labels stripped, filled from a large drum, he washes his head and feet, drinks what might be tainted, impure, he cannot know.

BARE

He kneels, lowers himself, touches his flat palms and forehead to the gray floor, the covering, the dirt. His prayers are birds, flying far from his lips.

CHAIN

Fastened to an iron bolt, the chain lets him reach the bucket-toilet, freights his body, he can raise his right hand no higher than his waist.

THE SOUND OF WAVES

The speakers blast music, then pause, and he listens for the call of a far mosque—then a recorded ocean, seagulls, waves breaking a shore.

Forever Prisoner

*At Guantánamo, indefinite detainees
are known as the forever prisoners.*

Carried to the feeding block by a forced cell
extraction team, laxative and vanilla Ensure
entering him through the tube in his nose,
tied to the restraint chair, he sees the photos
in *National Geographic* (mildewed, tattered)
he's pored over. He has by heart the gondolas
of Venice, can summon a teakwood dhow.

He doesn't vomit; the team carries him back.

In a cellblock in Camp 6, his ankles chained,
he stains cardboard with coffee, timbers
his clipper ship, ravels his prayer cap
for rigging, ties fine knots. While the anchor
(a bottle lid) grabs the sea-bottom, holds fast,
his rag-sails are ballooning with wind.

Simon Rodia Builds Nuestro Pueblo to Honor
His Brother Killed in a Coal Mining Accident

In steerage on the White Star Line, Simon
and his brother eat from the same pannikin,
share one hard bunk, across to the far country,

into the mines. When the props buckle,
when mules keen, the earth murmurs,
gives, enfolds, slams down,

and crushes his brother like an olive pit.
Alone, Simon must dig free, find light,
crawl to the mouth,

and blow ash from his hands. He moves
to Los Angeles, works for a cementer,
listens to jazz, guzzles wine, woos women,

and sheds each like a sweater
that scratches too much. Still a boy
with enflamed eyes, dust in his lungs,

he buys a weedy pie-slice of land
near the tracks in Watts. He drinks wine,
smashes the empties with a mattock, piles up

the glass-bits at the back of his lot,
a mountain of shine. He raises
a marker made of rebar,

chicken wire, and mortar; he adorns it
with shells, buttons, pebbles, corncobs,
the brightest shards. In dreams,

his marker becomes a tower
that spires into the sky,
its fragments catching light.

Praise House

1724

Where the river coils, snarls, changes aim,
they work the rice fields. Where the swamp-pools
stream back light and moss weeps low, they pour
the strength of their backs, break their bodies

to break clay, and raise banks to hold
off the river, dig ditches through raw woods,
open double trunks, let water sluice.
When the rice is in milk, May-birds pound

the air, blot the sun: a thick screech,
flapping wave. The people take up slings
and frails, knock bones. At moonrise, some go
to the groves, the burns, the ditches. Some

tap feet when the grandmother hums in shadows;
her daughter takes the people's woe, works it
into song; her grandson prays, lets the tongues
of water cool him, until *the morning star*

greets him there on his praying ground.

West Fork Glassworks

Clarksburg, West Virginia

In the hot room,
the finishing men
shape glass with pucellas
and shears. The snapper boy

tongs the gathers—
jars, jugs, flasks, and bottles—
into the crucible,
that they may become

pliant again. He carries them
to the bug-eyed finishers,
their loops and stems to be
flared and grooved.

Staring into the glory, he dizzies
and cries: there's a hot room
in the flames, smaller
than this, but brighter, molten,

wavering, with finishers
tweezing glass, and a bent boy
tonging for him
as he sways.

Self Portrait with Staghorn Berries

You skin bark-strips from the last
stick of birch, stray that I dropped
while I ran with kindling and reeds

from woodshed to groundhog kiln.
I feed the firebox, you salt your pots.
You're a panting thing, you're wound

like wire that bites soft pine, a nail
loose in the sawdust. If you want me
to keep you, you smooth your bristles,

ease your knots, and I'll be waxwing,
catbird, wheezing a scratchy tune
in the tangled hedgerow. Let me take

the cup of your scales, hips of rose,
sumac berries, the good of you
for my sustenance, crack and eat.

After Samson Burns Her Family's House and Grain-fields

Two charred bodies, galena-black, tar-black,
countenances gone. No ears, eyes, or lips.
Father, sister, offered to a god, fat and gorged,
that she deplores; hands folded
at the breastbone, as if fire was a balm
that soothed, gave them repose;
no hair to dress, no skin to wash and stroke.

Old moon when she sleeps, when she rises,
Nightjar's *karoo*, find a cave for her, interlunar,
the starless night through all her joints
and bones diffused, find scorched kernels
she'll gnaw from the stalk, find the burrow
where she'll hide, find water seeping
from stone, the fox that licks her hand.

What the Dust Drifts Down On

Kanawha County, West Virginia

His foam deer target, weed-choked corn stubble,
snaky pumpkin vines, the garden he fears

and the bed of mums, a thousand shriveled heads.
Martha's birdbath, concrete leprechaun. Blue poly tarp

spread over car parts—the Firebird a neighbor tree-wrapped
years ago. Smudged windows he cannot get clean

(she had a trick with newsprint and vinegar).
His land unfamiliar, rewritten, look for the dry well cap,

the empty creek—but animal bodies interrupt, another
dead goldfinch in the dogwood, wedged upright,

its head winter-gray, lifted, giving the testimony
of lung-clots. He ties a dated tag, lowers the finch

into his chest freezer, head tucked against breast,
slight in his hand, paper-wrapped, sealed in a plastic bag

from which he eased the extra air.

Red Notes

*after Eudora Welty's photograph "Tomato-packers' recess /
Copiah County / 1936"*

Tomatoes all day, unload the crates,
nozzle-wash each red Globe, each red
Bonny Best, feed them to the box of steam.
Tomatoes all day, he lugs full buckets
to the buzzards at the skinning tables.
His shift a blues, dirging on, note after note.

He hums, strings the notes,
fetches buckets, stacks the crates,
daydreams about *pies on a table.*
Her humming, his song on her lips,
a kiss blown through the steam
of corn in a pot, all the ears shucked.

Break-time on the stoop, work-shirts shucked,
the boys beg him to pick the notes,
play Worried Man Blues, play Waking Dream.
Break-time, the boys sit on crates,
offer him sandwiches, a pickled beet.
Not today. He piles crates for a table.

His head throbs. His guitar on the crate-table,
he rubs its sunburst body, plucks
one string, cry of a fox, small bruise.
His head throbs, and his hand. Not today. No notes.
Tomato worm stung him, ate
little holes in his palm. He dreams

she walks with him again, dreams
they find a keepsake for her vanity-table—
turkey feather, or arrowhead, or agate.
Before they meet, he'll wash with a bucket,
scrub the pulp off his hands, sing the notes
he's strung for her, tomato lonesome, tomato blue.

Rat-snakes in the holler, low-down blue,
he can see *a brass check for every bucket,*
each check a tooth bashed from the mouths
of the mummy-men at the skinning tables.
Pulp on his arms, the hissing steam,
notes he'll never sing, busted crate.

He hears the reds gossiping to the crates.
In the steam-fizzle, the bucket-clank,
the lies at the tables, he listens for notes.

Switchback

I'm the oxbow, flowing one way, then doubling back.
I'm the midnight itch, the crack in the patched rubber raft,

the petitions and pleas that come hissing out.
I'm the inflatable raven sitting atop the pizza joint.

I'm the mountain bike parked out front, the chafed
and carb-starved cyclist who sits on the bench and unscabs

his feet with a tack. I'm driftwood in the workshop,
hewn, lathed, and waxed. I run as I have never run,

veer from guardrail to ditch, trust the zigzags that climb
up to Briery Gap. I move like smoke through water.

The Pine Barrens

All night, flakes of ash blow into the barn, sift over
the cranberry pickers. He dreams about the tavern dance,
the woman who laughs and turns to sphagnum moss
under his touch, a chain of amber bubbles, sap blisters

on a blackened trunk. The next day, the bog owner
tells him to scout for salvage, sends him into danger.
Among tottering trees—swaying, crazed—he finds
a cluster of pines, charred but upright: the fire halted

where he cut breaks and plowed deep: his ragged scars
have warded off harm. His eyebrows singe. Ants cross
the smoldering needles at his feet, raise up sand-mounds,
do not falter until a sapsucker flashes down,

snatches a beakful. His skin prickles, flushes, blooms.
The cones ooze resin, open, and drop their seeds.

Camp Meeting in a Grove of Sycamore Trees

the preacher was an immensely tall and thin mountaineer

His mother says he's joe-pye-weed,
itching to grow. Too big for church,
he bumped his head on the ceiling,
goose-egged his crown the last time
he shouted there. Shirts don't fit him,
his ankles jut, jean cuffs creep up,
knobby wrists stick out. He stretches
while he sleeps: he's hammered tin.
In the clearing, he hangs torches
high in the trees, an easy reach;
he shouts glory, pumps his arms,
springs, then he floats among fireflies.
The spirit reels him up, dangles him
as he prophesies over the earth.

a mountain woman, in a gingham dress cut in one piece, rolled on her heels

At first, it's a labor. Her bones are heavy
as the tubs of sauerkraut whose lids
she weights with creek rocks.
The other women cry and sway.
She copies them: she waves her hands,
her arms, then her whole body shudders,
sweats, her hair comes loose.
When she gets the blessing, she drops
under the oaks, rolls over acorn shells
and dead leaves. She forgets sores,
burrs, blisters, muddy shoes, ugly things.
Freshets of new speech pour from her,
a dream that petals in her mouth.

once one steps off the State roads, the howl of holiness is heard in the woods

A brother swats the air as if hornets
fly too close. Then a sister brims,
shakes, and spills. Loose-jointed
as limberjack dolls, more brothers stomp
and flatfoot while the sisters testify,
hop over benches, weave with the frenzy
of honeybees smoked from the hive.
Tomorrow, one will pin herself
to the lines like a sheet the wind flaps
and fills. One will have a neck-crick,
buzzed lips, a hum on his skin.

Water Shrew as the Apostle Peter

The water shrew finds jetsam in his feeding pool
and larva-sized nubs of shattered glass
in the leaf mold. On the lip of the creek,

an old tin can that the shrew nudges
with his whiskery nose, that he frees
from the sedges and live-forever weeds.

Rusted to razor-lace, fine as a riffleshell,
the can holds little of the creek,
its indelible minerals, smorgasbord of debris.

What it holds—decaying vegetation,
a little silt—spills when the shrew jostles it.
Crepuscular in his habits, lissome

in his body when he dives
for the flatworm that he may
or may not find. Sheathed in air bubbles,

the shrew rises from the region of muck,
the compromised waters, and eyes the can
as it drifts, as the current has its way with it,

fragile craft. When caddisflies brush
the waters of his pool, the shrew catches
bubbles in his toe hairs—picture

pearly slippers, two pairs—then runs
the creek's surface, zags across the sheen.

Jarena Lee Preaches at Buffalo Village

Rain that pellets, ices the roof. At the hearth,
hulled corn soup, a Seneca woman who stirs
and stirs. Jarena Lee, lifting her arm

as if to pick from a tree and cup in her hand
some small golden fruit. As she testifies,
the interpreter speaks, holy flame runs,

and some Senecas weep, some cry amen.
Two tongues sing *o for thousands to know
the name*. When the spirit descends,

her bones quiver, she feels a mild sting,
the name that charms our fears, pulses
of heat streaking through her. To cross

sorrow's gulf, the few words that quicken.
God never forsakes. Milkweed strand,
silver hair, thread of a spider.

Looking for Creasy Greens in Late Winter
as Prayer of the Forsaken

Rulina rolls her sleeve, thrusts her arm in.
The icy creek-water makes her tremble,
chills her blood, needles her with stars of pain.
She churns her fingers, hears the water ring,
tumble over stones. Then some lower notes,
the suck of mud. No cress she might gather,
no mats of creek lettuce. She walks downstream,

punches holes in the creek, walks and punches
into the ice again. When her fingers stiffen,
when she can't make a fist, she strikes the ice
with the flat of her hand. The creek refuses,
will not answer, will not shatter. She holds
her ear to ice, the creek has no tongue now,
no flow. No game to shoot, no trout lilies,

no ramps, no tracks, no cone middens, no scat.
Under the ice-crusted beeches that glint
and drip, a jay pecks the meager snow, finds
not one stem or stalk. She gives it the heel,
the dab of lard from the pouch she brought.
Enough for a day, two days, if she bites small.
Rulina crosses broken fence, its rails sagging

or snow-snapped. She lays her rifle in snow
the color of trampled meal, then herself
alongside it. There is a shadow in her.
If she stays, she'll become a pillar of ice,
crystals that vanish on a warmer day,
away from the fevers of the log house,
the food whimpers, baby squalls, sour wash,

onion poultices smeared over the chests
of men. The older lame, fish-eyed. The younger
shiftless since his crop failed, his gun got wet,
fired wrong, flinted his face. *Dock and sorrel*
when spring comes, he says. *Make a meal of that.*
Father and son, widowers when Rulina met them,
thought it wise to pick the younger. *A good farm,*

he had lied, *plenty of everything. Near Mingo Rock,*
a church, a trade post. Plenty of sumacs,
hawthorns that tore Rulina's hands, ironweed,
and fifteen hard miles to Mingo Rock's
dead church, ghosted trade post. In her snow bed,
Rulina pictures *the creek as it loops,*
unspools, darts through the blind valley, sinks

into the cave mouth. Miles and miles underground,
she's heard, *running and running.* In her dreams
she goes into the creek as it slips down
to the earth's deeps, a dark ribbon she follows
by tallow-light, her mortal body wading
downstream, trailing behind her mirror-body,
body of silver, body of shimmer

that minnows pass through, minnows so pale
she sees traces of blood, red spider legs,
red smoke, the branching of the thinnest lines.
At the creek's outflow, she pours through, runs down
the next valley, runs the hollers, runs
beyond Yokum Ridge. Rulina rises
from the snow, shakes her iced hands, tries to stamp

her iced feet: she's a heavy stone. She trudges
upstream. Snow crunches underfoot; the sun hides;
the woods thicken and thin. A loud snort
startles her, her hands quiver. She bites her lip,
plants herself, holds her breath. Snow feathers down

25

from a shaken pine. She sees antler tips,
a flared nostril, then a bull elk appears,

sniffs, stops before the pine, browses the limbs.
First of his kind she's seen in ten years, rare,
lordly the way he holds his head, long-legged,
towering, the trees diminish behind him.
His undercoat is woolly, his rump-patch
creamy yellow, his winter shag the deep brown
of walnut dye. He stares at her with fierce eyes,

then he grunts, shakes his head, browses again.
Rulina studies his antlers, the maze of branches
and tines. Remembers the first squirrel she shot.
Remembers feeding her babies watery gravy,
corn-cakes thin as paper, roots limp as hair.
There is blood spray, the rifle-kick that knocks her
into the snow, the elk jerking, sinking

to his knees, and a cloud of steam. Later,
the men on their pallets will not get up
when Rulina returns. Fire almost out,
babies cheeping like birds, Rulina with blood
in her hair, burdened with all the meat.
Younger will say, *butcher in the full moon,*
else the meat will shrink. Older will say,

last herd I knew of kept to the barrens
west of Red Sulphur Springs, I was a boy.
Younger will say, *glad I taught you to shoot.*
Four squirrels your first day. Your good aim.
His fine talk has the weight of dandelion fluff.
She will feed him elk heart and liver, herbs,
yellowroot, strong kill-devil rum, he'll plow

when spring comes, she prays for this. She strains,
shoves, wedges her arms, gets the elk on his side.
His antlers snag in galax-vines. She cuts
his hide from the breastbone down, careful
not to pierce the guts. Ties leg-skins to haunches,
hangs them in the pine, and turns for home
with her dress full of meat. In the months ahead,

when the baby needs her milk that's dried up,
when the garden struggles, its few potatoes
no bigger than peas, she'll have some elk meat
she cured in the sun where none would find it,
her picture of the hidden creek, running
and running beneath the shell of the earth.

Grassy Branch Pentecostal Church

And now, tongue and groove, the lifting up,
yield, heads back, those who holler, let go.
Lard in the half-moon pies, two cups of flour,

self-rising. Sandals, steel-toes, crickets
under joists, ivy linoleum, Deward kneels,
swelling from the heat, wallboards shaven,

beaded joinings, curly maple, knotted pine.
Irish potatoes in the ridged-up earth,
eyes moving through the dark. The amen

caught in Hazel's throat, prayer language,
blood of the lamb, spirit touching spirit,
gush of vowels. Sweat inside a shirtsleeve,

an itch, tears blinked back, bearded iris bulbs
by the slab steps, greening the stony earth.

Near the ceiling, the face of Christ on tin
nailed up, it closes the gape where a stovepipe
passed into the wall. This sheet metal square
a rivet-punched messiah you hope will keep
out the winds, the griefs—with his thin beard
the color of puffball soot, multiflora rose
for a crown. His spooky eyes count the few
gathered here to cut out the prayer cloths,
to pat and squeeze their faith into the rags.
You brave blow-downs, the spreading ice.
Behind his dented tin, the cold howling night
could fray you bare. Holly-berries smashed
into his brow, this flea market savior hides
from you the absences, the ravenous hole.

Dish towels that he scalds in the speckled canner,
drives to the coin laundry for the dryers
(even the threadbare can be soft again).

That she irons, neatens, folds with lavender.

That they carry into church before the people arrive
and stack on the front bench—for footwashings,
for draping on the bare skin of the spirit-slain,
hairy ankles, varicose calves.

That she lifts from the floor
(scattered piles after the people leave)
and lowers into the basket he holds.

That ride in the truck cab, heaped up,
overflowing, between them, like a child.

the church's interior all rectangles,
plank benches, box organ, walls
the color of mushrooms or eggshells
ceiling of poplar, high, unadorned
whip-sawed, people waiting, heads
bowed, not moving yet, dry leaves

before the wind swirls, Bible stand
with wings on the sides, pitcher
and cups on one wing, peppermints
on the other, people with raised arms
open hands, bulbs hanging

from wires, no brightness
before the power comes
body as tabernacle, as ball jar
clean, bare, made ready
pressing along

when you stand with the men,
when you love, and do not despise,
and peel off Brother Ivan's moist socks—
his feet two toads, bumpy, swollen,
smelling of earth—his nails snaggled, pitted,
sandpapery, little buttons, little moons—
you dip his feet, wash, cradle, pat dry,
he says *oh*—and all of it—the water,
the soft pink towel, his pursed mouth,
skin on skin—is holy, holy, holy—

red maples shading the people who tuck in
with gusto at the sawhorse tables—

its hand-sized leaves breezing them
who have brought their appetites,
soft bellies, crow's feet, signs of decay—

sometimes dropping winged seeds
on the chocolate cream pie, the bowls
of potato salad, deviled eggs,
chow-chow, and the coffee urn,
the cobbler Brother Gilbert made
from a bushel of his beetled peaches
he could not sell

here's Sam Edes, he's backslided
all he can stand, he's in blaze orange,
unwashed, sour breath, he was headed for
the pines, the power cut, the deer blind
before he braked, yanked the wheel hard,
took the turn-off he had chosen against,
he'll still brag about the eight-point rack,
the tenderloin, but now the Holy Ghost
pulls him, at the altar rail your uncle pumps
his hand, bear-hugs him, he goes down fast,
spine of jelly, rags for bones, brightest
orange, shaking on his knees

One more time, the preacher draws
the tank-air through his oxygen hose
and rubber mask. He preaches, *shape us
on the potter's wheel,* he grunts,
he creaks like a rusty gate.
Mansions there, glorified bodies—ah.
He does that for you, you lean forward,
you amen, his words are as honeycomb,
as morels you reach for in the rich damp
of a decaying log. One more time,
the spirit gives him wind.

fill the lard cans, wild goose plums, river plums,
red June plums, mash them with your hands,
split the ruddy yellow-cheeked skins

break the bodies, do not crack the stones,
let the plums come under the power of boiling water
and yeast, set the plum mixture aside

seven days, let sugar and air move on the plums,
bubble and foam, set aside another seven days,
don't seal the cans too tightly

the spirit still has work to do, wait seven days,
and strain the pulp into the wide mouths,
the blue masons, the communion jugs

inside each a cloud, a ghost, a gloom

H. D. at Point Pleasant Beach

All evening the eelgrass slaps
its rough embroidery down

at the wrack-line, at damp sockets,
the moon-snails' methodical beds.
She loses count.

          Sleek grasses
pouring from the sea-maw, her breakers
like pitch pines. Tattered banners.
Slovenly tongues.

          Lamberton frets her hand,
offers his mackinaw.
Blue-lipped, she declines,
moves into the spray.

He hears her laugh, then only
the gabble of the waves.

Jawbone

We can throw songs instead of stones
from the dark wells rising in our throats.
We can make music with our bones,
with glass bowls and the bells of goats.

From the dark wells in our throats,
we mock him who tied the last sickled corn,
hang round his neck the bells of goats,
fix his hair with two stick-horns.

He who bound the last sheaves of corn
flees our hands, catches his breath,
tosses the bells and shakes out the horns.
With our bones, we deal the blows of death,

run from unclean hands, run out of breath.
Like the strongman with a jawbone club,
we mete with our bones the blows of death.
No strangers to grief, the bluesmen rub

the bleached teeth of jawbone clubs
with willow stalks, shake the teeth loose,
rattle their grief. Like the bluesmen, we rub
the blisters on our hands, swill corn juice,

chew sugar stalks till our teeth come loose.
We have no food unless we pick the ears.
With blisters on our hands, worm juice
on our flushed skin, we can't trick our fears.

We would starve without music in our ears.
We can throw songs instead of stones
to drive away the spirits we fear.
We can make music with our bones.

Sky Cathedral

> *My total conscious search in life has been for… the in-between places, the dawns and the dusks, the objective world, the heavenly spheres, the places between the land and the sea.*
>
> —*Louise Nevelson*

The filigree of balsa wood glued
in the splintery wine crate mimics
the angles of Nevelson's three a.m.

shadow as she carts home a hodgepodge
of staves, blocks, scraps, and newels
that she snagged, groping through

garbage cans and dumped goods,
wriggling her gloved hands.
At dawn, in her workroom, she dips

wood into troughs of matte black,
scroll-saws plywood to echo
Aztec glyphs, and sorts chair legs,

baseball bats, tenpins, and gunstocks.
She first composed with found wood
when her son was *in the war, at sea,*

in Egypt or Russia, it was secret,
she didn't hear from him six months
at a time. It threw her into despair.

The world was at war, and every son
was at war, and her work was black.
Cats with thumbtack eyes. The head

of a goddess. Now she won't lid, shut off,
or seal *Sky Cathedral*, her assemblage,
her sculpture, her all-black wall stack—

one crate framing dowels and knobs
like finch eggs in a juggler's pitch hands,
one crate a puzzle of cumulus clouds,

one a reliquary of fired bone shards,
some crates full of snaggleteeth
and canines, exhaling shadows

instead of breath.

Canaan Land

I. Judgment Day

Home from overseas, Kenny pawns his uniform, knife,
and dog tags. Catnaps on the bus. Old ladies read

rapture novels, kids fuss, the wheels lick the asphalt.
Four hours later, he lifts his duffel down from the rack,

walks to the farmhouse by the chapel.
Won't be there long. He smokes at the mailbox,

hunkers near the drifts, snow-buried yard gnomes
and fawns. Ava waves him in, picks

fuzz from her housecoat, lingers, won't touch him.
Before opening her present, she brings him coffee,

eggs like leather. She glares at the beggar-boy
carved from teak, recoils as if hornet-stung, drops

the idol in his lap, growls *take it back*.

II. After Her Husband's Wreck

The preacher went out to buy fake grass, toy sheep,
a long-life bulb for the manger; he hydroplaned,
slid into a post. At his funeral, his florist son

goes on about twisted metal, purple flesh;
the son in the army smells like blood and smoke.
Ava cuts the stars from apples, dismantles

cabbages, eats the clock gear by gear, sings
on my way to Canaan land, don't hinder me.
Her shoulders locked, her hair pulled back,

a tight knob. She admits the salesman who says,
show you something beautiful. A vacuum cleaner.
He plugs it in; they two-step with the circuits

of the wind. She gives him a fistful of blackberries,
the salt of her eye wetting his cheek, and the hours,
the years. She could powder him to flake and dust,

tooth and lash. He nods to her, packs the vacuum,
and takes it away. She's the blade, the stone,
she's the miller, the unwinder.

III. May Apples

In her mirror, Ava paints herself
as the old cheat's last plaything.
Her wilted celery look. She must lean

full-weight against the Dutch doors
that block her in, budge both halves
with her bony knees and wrists.

From the field, she harvests may apples
and bee balm, that she might boil
a cloudy tea for the preacher's bad back,

his fireless blood. He brightens,
springs from his chair, goes
out to feed his prize silver-laced

Wyandotte chickens, boasts to her
about the fair, crows about the spots,
dapples, and streaks of their feathers,

and naps again. From the woods,
she brings thin poplar rods,
peels the bark to expose the white

inner wood, lifts his head, and hides
the poplar under his pillow,
that he might be cured in his sleep.

He doesn't wake, sleeps open-mouthed.
In the closet, hangers scritch
as she swats them aside.

Like madcap birds, her hands
snatch and flail, yank out some sequined
diaphanous thing, and sail it around

45

her goosepimpled body.
She interrupts his shredded wheat;
he lowers his spoon. She pleads

give me a child;
he swallows, dabs his mouth
with the plaid napkin.

I'm not God, he says. She keeps trying;
opens pots, tubes, and tins;
chooses pale whispery stuff

to powder forehead and cheeks,
and for her mouth a burnt red
like the poppies she planted in a tire.

IV. Fireweed

Ava heard voices calling her, and she went
to the tabernacle, the house of prayer,
the harbor of souls, the holiness tent.
She got happy, ran the benches, spun like a top,
raced up the King's highway. She threw out
her horoscope, her lipstick, her garnet brooch.
Her neck pain was healed. She laid hands
on her cousin, and her cousin leaped up,
and shook off his steel brace. New words
spilled from her, they tasted like laughter,
like glittery bits of song. She saw the wind
playing the joe-pyes, goldenseal,
God drawing nigh. Her few holy
words tasting like the first blades
of grass in spring when she prays
in her garden, on the burnt ground
of her life, see now, she's fireweed

V. House with Two Exterior Doors

Front door writes down license plates.
With a brass monkey paw for a knocker
and its shadeless window face-sized,
front door staves off the sloping yard,
vine-throttled hills, power line buzz,
frackers' whine, and wings that rustle
like old bank notes. Front door holds
and will not spill the interior rooms,
periwinkle and dust-moted, the chests,
wardrobes, the preacher's typewriter
heavy as a smithy's forge,
firedogs, old mail drifting over counters,
and on the stove a kind of potato soup,
perpetually simmering. Add half-and-half
this evening, or bacon grease,
a clump of ramps tomorrow, if Ava refuses
the bread of idleness and goes out
through the front door,
ambles the deforested scrub-woods
and remembers the spade.

Balcony door squelches loose talk
that would seep out. Balcony door,
tight-lipped juror, hushes the second-story hall,
its cobwebs and lint, its paint in lizard-scales.
Given the cheep of hope pecking its shell,
she would pry up the nails, stand within
the balcony's iron petals till the outdoors
offered some gladsome sound: the maracas
of gravel churned under wheels, the cardinal's
countersong, the brush of dead ash leaves.
Storms felled that tree, unmoored the house,
left the balcony door groaning and askew;
hired hands stripped the balcony,
tamped the foundation down.
Take the vinyl poncho, cash for the merchant,
or trade the walnuts and pawpaws.
May nothing touch her, if she walks the ditch
or chances the shoulder to town,
if the sun shorts out,
if the sky pledges rain.

VI. Patchwork

The preacher's house another cast-off,
stuffed with ratty sofas, stacks of cord-bound
gospel tracts, rolls of tent canvas
and coiled guy-lines that barricade
the upstairs hall. Cardboard and blanket
squares taped to windows. Ava putters

from room to room, cuts his suits for a quilt,
passes his guitar to the garbage-man, burns
his sermons and balsa planes. Better to eat
cleaning-lye than to foul her mouth with the false
speech that pleased him, better to leave her church
than stay with him who hounded her to repent.

Each day she stuffs more holes,
casts out the chill, peels some green
from the wad of ones, mails the stepsons.
She nurses the sick aloe, boils bones
for carcass soup, feeds the tongues
of gold fire in the woodstove.

The Great Auks of Funk Island

Newfoundland

Drifts of kittiwakes still blizzard the islet,
a saturation of razorbills, a mercy of puffins.
Murres chatter to their eggs, brood on bare stone.

Long ago, men with bats drove the great auks
into corrals, boiled them in kettles. Snatched
their feathers for mattresses and pillows.
Left their meat to rot. None survives.

But look, there can be a flyaway chance, light
as sweater fuzz or hardtack crumbs, for creatures
to come here and hope. Think of the vagrant
black goose, and the naturalists who came,

freighted with wire skeins, barrels, and hoes.
Searching for remains, they found a jackpot,
under the guano and ash, thousands of bones.

The Wind Reports

She tells her son she fell reaching for her mailbox
that wasn't there. That the wind grabbed his card,
kited it down the street. That she blames the wind
on the draglines eating the hills. That nothing
looks right; where neighbors' houses should be,
she sees ironweed, foundation holes. That the wind
over the rubble of the Guyandottes roars like
a rain-swollen creek. That she won't sell or leave.
That the wind smacks the moon-sized rock above
her house, inches it toward the lip of the ridge.

She doesn't tell anyone her house whimpers.
That the electric candles on her sills pass messages
to airplanes. That the hills look like Molly's busted
crayons, broken nubs. That she sings *dry bones*
over and over. That vireo eggs are her kindred—
dotted, red-eyed, sure to crack if unnested.

Mouthful

Creek a murmur, moon a dim button,
gurgle of water, soft wash of light,
encampment. After the skirmishes.
Under buffalo skins, hickory withes,
all of us spent, poured out, limbs
around trunks, haunch against shank,
curled together. Fern fronds,
bean vines. After the raids. Chew on
haws and roots, trust in fox-grapes
not yet seen, maypops, creasy greens,
groundfalls. Through stone beds,
muddy pools, we drag our boats,
repeat the cries. May spirit-groans spill
from our lips, may streaks of mercy
flare up, sear through lids we close,
through skies we bitter with our breath.

Mary of Bethany

She dips her shaky fingers
in juglets of aloe, sweet cane,
spikenard; she rinses the moon jar;
like tally marks in the copper tray,
she arrays the pins pulled loose

to spill her hair on his feet;
she presses coriander leaves
to her puffy eyes. In her hands,
the feel of his dirty feet, grass-flecked
right, dung-crusted left, his feet

the color of honey or new bronze
as she scrubbed and oiled them,
his burnished feet she wetted
with tears and kisses, holy feet
she wiped with the fall

of her hair. In his thudding footsteps,
she heard and did not believe
the convulsing of the temple
that was to come, the crack of flame.

Travels in Mali

He loosens his throat and murmurs as the bus
reaches the market, grinds its brakes.
He discards the rumors of pickpockets,
tourists pelted by wire-thin boys.
If prayer could be the cool smooth stone
he keeps close. If he puts down his backpack,
rents a room. If he stays.

The tallest building a mud-walled mosque,
tannish-yellow, the color of so much here:
camels he crosses the street to dodge, the sky,
the porridge and fried plantains he buys from
a woman sitting at a table of covered bowls.

If he climbs to the mosque's rooftop, takes in
a copper sunset, the river's distant gleam.

The guard blocks him: foreigners are not welcome
in the holy place.

He ducks his head, turns to go, steps around
the jug-toting women, the children playing
with pebbles, furrowing the dust.
If he gets to silence, makes a small cell
or interval of it. May there be aloe
and myrrh for the hurt, and kindness
when strangers eye each other on the street,
and enough darkness, enough light.

*

The drums made from antelope skin
clatter on the piecemeal stage.
He wants to flee, his skull throbs
from the bush taxi, the too-much sun,
the not-enough safe water
in the bottle half-full and too-soon-gone.

Then three Tuareg metalsmiths strike drums
like striped barrels—their arms frenzied,
whip-like, untiring—and he forgets to leave,
he loosens, with the fairgoers, he sways.

Nomad women with silver-wrapped fingers
pound drums that are smaller, more slender.
Drums anointed, his guidebook says,
with a tuning paste of soot and goat fat.

The women slap their drums, cradle them,
swing them high.

If he could pour out his treasures,
let his life flow, awake to all things,
singing of the weal and the woe.

As one drum joins its rhythm to the din,
so he wants to add what he can give
to the fury and the fray.

Karst Country

Bats feasting in our back pasture,
in the stubble-fields on nights of swelter,
mosquito-drone, sheets thrown back.
Under our pasture, flow paths,

and rimstone pools, and chambers branching,
sponge-like, ramiform—a world where
the sun is a parable, the flowers are stones.
That world—breathing on us in fields rumpled

and laced with fissures, caverns, and pits—
sends us bats as emissaries: pipistrelles,
big-eared, Eastern red, some silver-haired,
some "smoke-colored, deepening to black,"

as Graceanna Lewis observes. Furless,
their wing-membranes are "crimped by lines
of blood, like the India crape dresses worn
by our mothers." Bats threatened by our smoke,

our dirt. Isaac Weld recalls: Madison's Cave
was "soot-covered from the pine torches"
carried by guides, its petrifactions grimy;
his "hands and clothes were smutted over."

Juice smears our faces when we eat blackberries
with abandon. We learn the pleasures of tasting,
of savoring. Of new hay, that clovery smell.
Finches harvesting hemlock seeds. Bats feeding

on moths. And water that gnaws stone.

Brush Arbor

Sandstone cliffs, then the woods again
where I come to a stand of redbuds, *no-da-tsi*,
blooming Judas, trees that bleed
in the spring, corner posts of the brush arbor
where the believers tremble and call out.

Listen to the big-lunged,
the reborn, wren song and owl testimony,
peeper trill.

All will diminish, burn away,
greenbriers will choke the arbor,
pull it down, and tongues grow moss,
prophecies go dry, our days as foamflowers,
hepaticas that shatter, stems that break.

Say it plain, I tell myself. That in the hollows,
in the gaps, you believe.

Self Portrait on the Blackwater Trail

Soon, the loggers will slash the hardwoods
and red spruce, drive the flying squirrels

from their woodpecker holes, tree cavities,
spare no homes. Near the old coke ovens,

the gutted seams, I enter the woods, sprawl
under a birch, its leaf mold printing my skin.

Clifton said: *earth is a black shambling bear.*
Kumin said: *the soul of the chopped beech*

flies into air. If I could see like that, I'd stay
with the spruce, declare I'm part-squirrel,

feed on lichens, leap from a spruce crown,
leap like I was made for it, and then glide.

Alternate Take on Scenes from Beneath the Underdog: His World as *Composed by Mingus*

On the Sears trombone, on his sister's piano,
on the double bass, he tries *to play the truth*
of what he knows: his father shooting pigeons

from the sky, swinging his fists, his strap—
and the Duke's Toodle-Oo and Creole Love Call
frying on the radio—and *the blues of the Holiness*

prayer meetings his stepmother takes him to,
the church-folks *in trances, their riffs and moans*—
the backyard garden, its chickens, and fig tree,

and greens—and the girl he kisses by movie-flicker
at the Largo—the seashells, busted dinner plates,
tiles, and glass he sells for pennies to Simon,

the cranky old man on 107th, who presses them into
cement birdbaths and towers—and taco stands,
the Japanese grocery, and Junkman Sander's

fighting yard—and the rubber balls he squeezes
to strengthen his hands—and Simon *changing ideas*
as he works, taking down what displeases him,

so that pinnacles two stories tall rise up, vanish,
and rise again—and the sharps and beats,
the rosin that gives grip to his horsehair bow.

American Taliban: Two Photographs

This photo is *official, surveillant, the A-team's*
routine effort, taken after he was seized with
a bullet in his thigh, hooded, stripped naked,
duct-taped to a gurney, sealed inside a metal
shipping box, let out when the team pressed
him for truth: he'd renounced San Anselmo,
the redwoods, his hip hop CDs, he'd taken in
like food the surah, the rhythmic prose, gone
to a language madrasa, a training camp,
hidden in a basement that the Alliance flooded
with a diverted irrigation ditch. Another photo,
printed out, pinned to my wall, his fervent eyes
on me as I sit on the floor, his robes the bright
of bleached sand. I try to pray with my pulse,
my guts stirring, not the same old speech.
The distance between us shifts. I listen for
his breaths, ragged and uneven.

Congregations

Harlan County, Kentucky

Sometimes I still sense the gatherings here,
eleven years after the road crews pulled down
Crummies Holiness Church, where the faithful
washed feet, shook tambourines, and prayed

all at once—a tide of voices that washed in,
dropped down, crested again, the long and low
church—red-brick, tarpaper—converted
from a bathhouse where miners sang

Over Yonder and Sour Apple Tree
as they scoured their bodies to quicksilver,
the bathhouse built in a field with a lick
where buffalo are said to have grazed—

congregations whose snorts and moans,
I almost hear—the beseechments,
the praise—whose heat and mass
I almost feel, then know as gone.

Self Portrait with Electric Oscillating Fan

I'm sitting in the back at Grassy Branch
when the anointing falls, a wind that hits,
stirs up, limbers nearly everyone, some sway
like dogwoods, sail down the aisles, crumple
in heaps, the church reels, Sister Mae
testifies, there is crying and hollering
that rises, rises, then recedes, there is hush,
faint sobbing, I hear the still small
voice of the electric oscillating fan,
the buzz that stirs the stale air, *do this*
it says, *abide* it says, it cools the back
of my neck a moment, then it turns
and I nearly flee this ravished place
I smell wood, the walls trapping heat,
the pine benches, the sap, I smell bodies,
sweat, dark circles, the men damp,
the women damp, a trace of Ivory soap,
bodies that work with coal and slate,
deer meat and grease, bodies that smell
like their work, hand over my nose
I smell them stronger, *them a part*
of me, they are me now, the still small
hum of the fan again, the stirring,
the cool, while it hums on me, I stay

Chorus Frog

The season of cracking open, bloodroot,
egg strings. My grandmother chops the cloddy
ground. Many years without him. Onion sets,
new moon peas. Frogs in the pond they sank in,
shearing cattails below the waterline. Frogs
an inch long, a blue-ash color, dark stripes,
sunning on sunken logs, *on tussocks, swimming
among floating debris.* Pour out, swell up,
jewelweed and monkey flower. She hears frogs
calling, a rattle that pitches up, up, *a scraping
coarse-toothed comb.* Waiting to follow him.
How many. She lists, snags, thins. All the time
she tries to catch a ballad, plaint, what he sings
from the next, the after.

Spring Up Everlasting

from sinkhole, wash-out, cascade
that sheets a cliff-face; glisten us
when we peel off work shirts
and overalls. Ease these fears

of subsidence and dam-bust.
Counter the wind that scours
those who come from whippings
and revivals; dissipate the fog

that bewilders dump trucks
and six-tons. Let down droplets
that xylophone a cave floor.
When storms rattle the pin-oaks,

when the sky is a bruise, give us
the smell of a pawpaw so ripe
it splits, a waterpot of spirit
and truth, a flushed-out creek.

Warn us when the hour comes
for a bubbling-up, a brimming-
over of cistern, or basement,
or stream, that we may bring

buckets, canning jars, our leaky
hands, and fill them with some pitch,
some slurry, and turn back the tarry
waters rising at our feet.

Acknowledgments

For first publishing the individual poems of *Spring Up Everlasting*, I thank *Alaska Quarterly Review*, *America: The Jesuit Review*, *Appalachian Heritage*, *Cerise Press*, *The Christian Century*, *Confrontation Magazine*, *Construction*, *Hayden's Ferry Review*, *The Missouri Review*, *North Dakota Review*, *Notre Dame Review*, *Presence: A Journal of Catholic Poetry*, *Radar Poetry*, *River Styx*, *Saint Katherine Review*, *Still: The Journal*, *storySouth*, *Southern Humanities Review*, *Southwest Review*, *The Threepenny Review*, and *West Branch*.

In writing *Spring Up Everlasting* I consulted many sources from which occasional phrases were taken or adapted.

About the Author

William Woolfitt is the author of two other books of poetry, *Beauty Strip* (Texas Review Press, 2014) and *Charles of the Desert* (Paraclete Press, 2016), and also a fiction chapbook, *The Boy with Fire in His Mouth* (Epiphany Editions, 2014). His short stories, poems, and essays have appeared in *Tin House*, *The Threepenny Review*, *African American Review*, *Shenandoah*, *Michigan Quarterly Review*, *Colorado Review*, *Epoch*, *The Cincinnati Review*, *Image*, and elsewhere. He has received a Howard Nemerov Scholarship from the Sewanee Writers' Conference and two Denny C. Plattner Awards from *Appalachian Heritage*. He teaches creative writing and literature at Lee University in Cleveland, Tennessee.